PORTFOLIO B

METROPOLITAN SEMINARS IN ART

Great Periods in Painting

PORTFOLIO B

Earth, Heaven, and Hell

MAN AND MYSTERY IN THE MIDDLE AGES

BY JOHN CANADAY

ART EDITOR AND CRITIC
THE NEW YORK TIMES

THE METROPOLITAN MUSEUM OF ART

EARTH, HEAVEN, AND HELL

Man and Mystery in the Middle Ages

HISTORY seldom wraps itself into neat parcels while it is happening. Historians divide the story of the world into chapters later on, at a safe distance from the events. In devoting all but the last few paragraphs of the preceding portfolio to Greece and Rome and giving over all but the first few of this one to the flowering of Christian art after the year 1000, we may seem to imply that classical antiquity stopped at the end of one chapter in time and that the Christian world began, just as suddenly, on the first page of another.

But if Rome was not built in a day, neither did it fall in a day, a year, or a century. The seven hundred years following the convenient date of 313, the year the Roman emperor Constantine legalized Christianity, were centuries when Rome as a state faded and Rome as a way of thought gradually lost its identity, merging with and coloring Christianity. During these centuries Christianity as we know it was developing out of the Eastern cult it was when people first turned to it for solace as the gods of Rome failed them.

The history of these centuries is extremely complex in events and in art. Our purpose here is to discuss only those cultural mainstreams that have been most directly tributaries to the art that is part of our lives—meaning, in this case, that we will just glance at the semioriental art of the Byzantine Empire.

In the preceding portfolio we saw the Byzantine mosaic *Saint Agnes* (Plate A10) from Ravenna, Byzantium's western outpost in Italy. This mosaic, with its golden background, its stiffness, and its flat, decorative character approaching abstract pattern, will have to represent for us the formalism of the Byzantine style when we refer to its reflection in later pictorial art.

The Byzantine style spread to Europe and, combined with local traditional styles, took root in the monasteries of Germany, France, and England—a northern world that was still half barbarian. Within the protective isolation of the monasteries the illuminated manuscript became a depository of art and culture awaiting rebirth.

This rebirth very nearly occurred around 800 under Charlemagne, who for a few years gave Europe the first political unity it had had since Rome. But after Charlemagne's death his empire dissolved under multiple misfortunes.

The Year 1000

Then, shortly after the year 1000, Europe began to stir with new life. According to an appealing explanation this happened because the end of the world, scheduled in apocalyptic prophecies for the millennium, failed to occur; so people decided to carry on and make something of a world that apparently had another thousand years to go. Unfortunately there is no support for this convenient explanation; the true one is less engaging but more reasonable: by the year 1000 Europe had reorganized itself into the feudal system of manors and monasteries, a new political system that supplied the stability and permitted the accumulation of wealth necessary for the revitalization of a civilization that had all but died.

Now some miraculous process of germination seemed to be taking place in the soil; buildings began to grow from it in new abundance, low and heavy at first but rapidly gaining in height and grace. It was as if gigantic seeds of stone had sprouted and thrust up into the light new and wonderful forms, fantastic stone stalks unlike anything ever seen before. Increasing in complexity as they spread and flourished, they became the piers and columns of the great churches of the Middle Ages. They opened out at the top into webs of arches (*Figure 1*), the skeleton of vaults that hovered ever higher and higher in the air. And above the buildings' mass, even higher than the vaults, towers rose, extended by spires tapering to points far above the earth, seeming to merge with the sky.

These churches blossomed everywhere with sculpture in shapes of angels, kings, saints, demons, and common people. Abbot Suger of Saint Denis in Paris, who planned his own church and signed its portal, brought to a climax the conception of the ecclesiastical building as a pedagogical medium. Saint Denis was a prototype for later churches, which became vast stone encyclopedias summarizing all knowledge in systems of images and symbols—reflecting the life of man on earth, serving as his guide to the hope of heaven, and warning him of damnation in hell. The sculpture told the story of man and the world and explained it according to the "four mirrors" of the *Speculum majus*, a supreme effort of medieval learning. The mirror of nature described the creation of the world, including man, the plants, and the beasts, both real and imaginary; the mirror of morals contrasted virtues with their corresponding vices; the mirror of instruction told of man's work, manual and intellectual, from ploughing and harvesting to

Archives Photographiques, Paris

Figure 1

mathematics and music; the mirror of history outlined the story of man, sacred and profane, from the day of his creation to the Last Judgment. Wherever possible—on portals, on capitals, on spires, in bands across the façade—the cathedral carried sculpture that told the story of the Old and New Testaments and illustrated the Christian idea of salvation, showing the joys of the blessed and the tortures of the damned. There were images of humility and pride, prudence and folly, pilgrims and students, dancing goats and fighting birds, mythical monsters and Christian saints, pygmies and giants, carpenters and artists, Hercules and Moses, lovers and murderers—all united as parts or symbols of a religious scheme. The Nativity might be represented on one hand, a droll fable on the other. The sculptors were not afraid to use humor, as in the image of a knight dropping his sword in fright as a rabbit jumps out of a nearby bush (*Figure 2*), a more telling symbol of cowardice than a high-flown allegorical figure might have been.

The complexity of the cathedral was unified

6

by the element that gave meaning to all the contradictory variety of medieval life. This element was faith, faith that the universe of earth, heaven, and hell was organized according to the divine purpose of God. The cathedral was the tangible expression of medieval man's faith in divine intangibles, the rational and material form in which he symbolized the nonrational basis of Christian revelation. This logical expression of mystical faith is a contradiction, but this very contradiction completed the identification of the cathedral with medieval philosophy, which began with the premise of revelation, then contradictorily sought to demonstrate the mystery of God through logical systems.

Our discussion will be limited largely to French sculpture and architecture, because, most people would admit, the medieval spirit received its consummate expression in France.

Sculpture: the Linear Style

The traditions of monumental sculpture had virtually disappeared when the eruption of ecclesiastical building began to require sculpture in great quantities for the first time since Rome. When the medieval stone carvers—we may begin to call them sculptors—were called on to create entire portals, as well as capitals and freestanding statues, they turned for ideas to whatever sources were available.

The richest mine was the illuminated manuscript, which had already served as a source for ivory carvers. Now whole schools of sculpture developed under its influence, presenting the anomaly of a monumental art translated from a miniature one, the contradiction of hard stone carved in the kind of line usually struck in quickly with the tip of a fine brush.

The tympanum of the narthex of the church of Saint Madeleine at Vézelay (*Figure 3*) is designed in this linear style. From the hands of a gigantic figure of Christ, rays of pentecostal fire descend on the heads of the apostles, who are portrayed in the bent, twisted, dancing at-

titudes by which the sculptor, like the illuminator, animated his figures. The apostles are to carry the gospel to the far corners of the earth; thus, on the lintel and on the inner semicircular band above it we see all the peoples of the world, including the dog-headed men who were supposed to inhabit India and others with ears as large as wings. All of them, according to the prophecy of the church fathers, will be included in the universal conversion to Christianity; some of them, like the three small figures who show one another their once-lame legs, have already been converted through miraculous cures.

The Vézelay tympanum is a spectacular and impressive composition, far more than a mere copybook exercise translating a manuscript illumination into a new medium. The patterned lines are half abstract, in the Byzantine tradition, and are extraordinarily elegant as pure design. But additionally, Christ (*Figure 4*) is a figure of grandeur, electric with the power of the spirit. The fluttering, swirling rhythms flame with energy, as if the stone had an inner force that charged the carved images.

Bildarchiv Foto Marburg

Figure 2

7

Figure 3

Realism

But sculptors discovered a source of inspiration that in the end proved to be more important than manuscripts, ivory carvings, or fragments of antiquity. This source was the world itself, offering its people and plants and animals and places and things to be observed and studied; this world, which, as God's creation, was the natural source for images telling of His word; the world of which Saint Francis sang with such joy that he revealed it to the Middle Ages as a miracle, at hand, to be loved.

Linear formalism and observant realism developed side by side; they could even coexist in a single piece of sculpture. A lovely *Virgin and Child* (Plate B1) from Auvergne, a part of France where the linear style sometimes became extreme, has obvious conventionalizations of that style in the drapery, but the face of the Virgin blends life with formula. Sharp lines have begun to give way to sculpturally conceived forms inspired by the look of human features; there is an effort to give natural shape to the strong jaw and chin, to suggest bones

beneath the cheeks. The life in the Vézelay sculpture is synthesized by expert manipulation of a crystallized style, but the life in the face of the Auvergne Virgin comes from the sculptor's determination to capture its quality as he observed it.

The face of the child, with its staring Byzantine eyes and generally flat look, is more conventional. Sculptors and painters of all early schools seem to have found it difficult to represent children except as little old men. Or possibly the sculptor was more timid here. It may very well be that he did not feel free, or did not feel urged, to humanize the holy child as he did the Virgin, who was becoming the sweet and compassionate figure of Our Lady.

The Tympanum at Conques

The tympanum of the church of Saint Foy (*Figure 5*) in the village of Conques in southern France is warm, solid, and human, at least in comparison with the abstract agitations of the one at Vézelay, although the two are of about the same date.

8

The subject of the tympanum is the Last Judgment. Approaching Christ on his right hand is a row of figures suggesting a file of pilgrims (*Figure 6*). The Virgin, leading, is followed by Saint Peter, conspicuously identified by his key, and Saint James of Compostela, at whose church in Spain the Way of Saint James, which passes through Conques, terminates. After him, a bishop leads a king by the hand, the bishop firm and self-assured, the king bearing a scepter, the symbol of his power, but stooping a bit, for kings made pilgrimages with all the humility of common people.

These personalities are vividly real, vividly characterized in face and attitude. These are real people instead of animated effigies; their robes fall naturally instead of fluttering and twisting in arbitrary patterns. The figure of Christ, appropriately more formalized than the others, is thus separated in heavenly majesty, but even here, in comparison with the Christ at Vézelay, there are strong realistic references.

The Conques tympanum is one of the most direct and satisfactory organizations of a large area in the history of sculpture. Dozens of figures are accommodated without confusion or monotony in episodes described detail by detail. Essentially this was done by subdividing the area. This device would have been too obvious if the dividing bands had not served also as descriptive legends so beautifully designed that they become important parts of the scheme. The divisions might still have been monotonous if at the bottom they had not been peaked on either side, on the left as a palace representing Paradise and on the right by a similar gable under which the damned are being punished. These pointed bands are repeated, but varied, by the angles of the scrolls carried by the angels to the left of Christ.

When the major divisions were established, the sculptor was left with some awkward minor spaces to fill—long, narrow, triangular areas that should have presented difficulties. Most designers would have settled for a little ornament here, but this artist was not willing to

waste a fraction of his space on pure decoration. The pointed shape above the palace of Paradise (lower right, *Figure 6*) is deftly used to accommodate the episode of the resurrection of the dead. A closed coffin fills the narrowest, most awkward part. As the space widens, a head and hand emerge from a second coffin as an angel lifts the lid. Next, in a still more generous width, a figure rises high enough to get his arm and shoulders outside the coffin. The process continues in a third group. Altogether, the series creates an impression of progressive action so perfectly adapted to the space available that the space might seem to have been created to accommodate the composition, rather than the other way around.

In the corresponding triangle (lower left, *Figure 6*) the narrowest portion is filled with the hand of God reaching from the clouds to receive Saint Foy, to whom the church at Conques is dedicated. She emerges from an arched building representing her church, in which (just visible in *Figure 5*) some chains hang. Saint Foy was the patron saint of prisoners; many who were released after prayers to her

Editions Tel

Figure 4

9

Figure 5

made pilgrimages to Conques and left their chains as votive offerings. Some of these chains still hang in the church of Saint Foy today.

Romanesque and Gothic

The Conques tympanum and the one at Véze-lay are masterpieces in contrasting styles, realistic and linear. Realism was finally to predominate over the mannerism of the linear style as Romanesque sculpture merged into fully developed Gothic.

"Romanesque" designates the medieval period from about 1000 to about 1200; "Gothic," the period from 1200 to about 1400 in Italy, or to about 1500 in northern Europe. Neither term is descriptively accurate. There is nothing very Roman about most Romanesque art except that the roundheaded arch, which was also used by the Romans, is typical of most Romanesque structures. "Gothic" is even less appropriate, implying a barbarian character in an art that actually included vestiges of barbarian ornament only as a fractional fraction

of its total vocabulary. Even the term "Middle Ages" is unsatisfactory if we look at it twice, suggesting that these wonderful centuries were nothing more than way stations in the transition from antiquity to the modern world.

It would be too bad to leave the period without also seeing a minor sculptural work or two, like the paired capitals (*Figure 7*) carved by an obscure master for the cloister of the abbey of Saint-Guilhem-le-Désert. One of the joys of Romanesque art is that its lesser monuments, even fragments of them, have the same vitality, invention, and ingenuity as the major ones.

In Greece and Rome the capital was a repeated form, identical from column to column, and its carving was purely ornamental. For the Romanesque sculptor each capital was a new problem, a new obligation to tell a story clearly, or at least an opportunity to invent new combinations of ornamental detail. The acanthus leaves on the capitals from Saint-Guilhem-le-Désert have been crisply and ornamentally carved; above, on the abacus block, there is a fanciful adaptation of a vine motive twining

10

around a series of heads. These elements, though classical in origin, are combined with happy enthusiasm rather than classical restraint.

Another capital (*Figure 8*) from the same cloister shows the damned being herded into hell mouth. The special compositional interest lies in the typical ingenuity with which a required subject is adapted to a difficult space. The salient corner is defined by a delighted demon who thrusts a poor naked mortal head-first into the yawning jaws of a monster, from whose mouth flames curl upward around the grimacing heads of other unfortunates. The elements—twisting fire, patterned teeth, heads, and bodies—are combined in ways that recognize the shape of the assigned space, in this case an outward-flaring, four-sided one, yet every element is effective didactically. This, after all,

is not much less than we have said about the important and complicated work at Conques.

Chartres: the Royal Portal

Romanesque sculpture reached its climax and Gothic sculpture had its beginning in the figures of the Royal Portal (*Figure 9*), the west entrance of the cathedral of Notre Dame at Chartres. These regal personages are called the Kings and Queens of Judah, the ancestors of Christ, although there are questions about this identification.

The tympanums at Vézelay and Conques are sculptural compositions in architectural frames, but the Kings and Queens of Judah are themselves half architectural. The extreme elongation is less a matter of style than of architectural integration. The figures occupy their posi-

Figure 6

Figure 7

Figure 8

tions logically, like columns—which they suggest (*Figure 10*). The pleats in the skirt of a queen resemble a column's channels; her long braids, the folds of her garments, and her upper arms are kept to architectural verticals. The flow of other lines, curved or slanting, is always drawn into the strong vertical pattern of the figures and of the architecture as a whole.

The figures as they are arranged today, bordering the triple entrance of the portal, are sometimes a little ragged, a little pinched. We do not know the original scheme, but when the body of the church was rebuilt following a fire in 1194, the portal was moved forward to a slightly smaller space between the towers. The portal may be a little undersized in relation to the whole façade, but the Kings and Queens of Judah remain supreme examples of architectural sculpture.

If they were nothing more they would be important, but in addition they are, by themselves, masterpieces of expressive art. Ranged in hieratic dignity, they are as compassionate as they are noble, as warmly alive as they are dignified and reserved. They combine the decorative verve of the linear style with a new architectural discipline and add to it a lyrical humanism and a plastic quality. If the unknown masters who carved the heads did not work from models (as they may have done), they certainly had studied the structure of faces, the lift of cheekbones, the set of a mouth

in the muscles alongside it, the depth of the eye socket, and the disposition of the lid over the eyeball with a knowledge and understanding only hinted at until now (*Figure 11*).

By usual judgments the Royal Portal precedes the full flowering of medieval sculpture and occupies a historical position comparable to that of Greek sculpture just before the supreme Parthenon pediments. It is true that a little later Gothic sculpture goes beyond the Kings and Queens of Judah in fullness and grace, that occasionally these figures cling a little precariously to their architectural framework, and even that there are some awkward figures among them. But there are not many medievalists who would be willing to sacrifice the Royal Portal for any other group of medieval sculptures. The complexity of the Middle Ages denied it the one supreme and total expression the Parthenon gave to the Golden Age of Greece, but the medieval world came closest to receiving that expression at Chartres, in the cathedral where the Royal Portal embraces those who come to enter it.

The Architecture of Chartres

Like some other cathedrals Chartres was built over such a long period of time that it encompasses several styles. A medieval architect taking up interrupted work never thought of continuing to build "in style." Old plans were

12

abandoned and new work was done in a contemporary style. Most of the façade of Chartres (*Figure 12*), like the Royal Portal that is a part of it, is late Romanesque or early Gothic, as you wish—Romanesque in its flatness and severity, Gothic in its vertical emphasis. But years and a long stylistic development separate the two towers of Chartres. The spire of the north tower, lacy, delicate, and elaborate, was built (1506–1512) when the Gothic style was being pushed to its limits. It strikes most people as disharmonious with the earlier tower (1180–1194), but it is brought into harmony by its greater height, which balances the (apparently) greater weight of its companion. Between 1194 and 1260 the body of the cathedral behind the western façade was built in purest Gothic style, just before the development of those extraneous elaborations and exaggerations typical of late stages.

One passes through the embracing Royal Portal from daylight into deep twilight, where stained-glass windows are suspended like curtains of colored light. After a few moments the piers begin to emerge, rising upward and upward into the shadowy recesses of stone vaults that seem to hover weightlessly, denying the reality of material things, declaring the greater reality of the spirit.

For medieval man space was the symbol of God; therefore, the history of cathedral architecture is the history of the creation of space, not as practical necessity (although the accommodation of large congregations was a factor) but as a mystical expression. This creation was made possible by the pointed arch, or vault, and the flying buttress. But, besides its structural advantages, the pointed vault satisfied esthetic and expressive needs. It not only permitted the lifting of vaults to greater heights but its pointed shape increased the impression of height. The roundheaded Romanesque vault (*Figure 13*), a single curve that moves upward and then turns back toward earth, seems

Figure 9

to say that man cannot escape this world; the apex of the Gothic arch is the climax of two upward movements that point toward heaven, suggesting the union of man's spirit with God.

To create space the Gothic builders invented some of the most daring engineering forms in history. Gothic cathedrals are not supported by their walls; the walls are mere skins of stone and glass stretched between members of an ingeniously devised skeleton. The vaults spring from piers too slender to support them; piers heavy enough to do so would have been ponderous, ungainly violations of the space through which they rose. The vaults are supported from the outside by flying buttresses that leap to meet them (*Figure 14*). The Gothic cathedral is an enormous ribbed cage in which no part is self-supporting. Every part is held in balance by another part; buttress and vault support one another in a system of thrust and counterthrust, a wonderfully logical system for the creation of the mystery of space.

Stained Glass

When the stained-glass windows of Chartres were removed for safekeeping during the two World Wars, the effect was to reveal a stunning example of engineering in stone emptied of the spirituality that made it the climactic summation of medieval mysticism and one of the supreme expressions of the human spirit. For the purpose of stained glass, in addition to its ornamental and storytelling functions, was not to admit light but to control it, to control the degree and the quality of light in space. Here and there, when the sun strikes directly through a window, brilliant colors may be thrown against a pier or a bit of floor, but these dramatic patches, moving and soon fading, are isolated in a vibrant half-light that half reveals, half conceals, the forms of soaring stone.

The cathedral's windows, like its sculpture, were part of a pedagogical scheme. One of the finest windows at Chartres (detail, Plate B2), if a single one can be chosen from so many, tells the story of the Roman general Placidas, his conversion to Christianity, and the events of his life leading to sainthood.

The story reads upward from the bottom. In the square medallion at lower center Placidas hunts the stag. His huntsmen and hounds flank him in the smaller medallions at either side. In the circular medallion at upper left a cross appears to Placidas between a stag's antlers, a miracle that caused the pagan general's conversion. In the medallion at the right he is baptized and takes the name Eustace.

Just above, if we could follow the window, we would come upon small medallions of furriers and clothiers busy at their crafts. The sudden interpolation of these good guildsmen in the story of Saint Eustace is easily explained: they contributed the funds for the

Houvet

Figure 10

14

Archives Photographiques, Paris

Figure 11

window. The inclusion of these ordinary people is interesting enough as a signature, but it is more significant as an expression of a way of thought in which the most ordinary, everyday things could appear unquestioned in the company of holy ones.

The considerable attention we gave to pictorial composition in previous portfolios should help to show how skillfully the designer has met the special problems involved in the famous medallion of Placidas' vision of the cross. Limited to a small circular shape and working with chunks of glass (for the glass of medieval windows is not the smooth, flat glass we know today), the artist had to show horse and rider, dogs, trees, antlered stag, and cross. He did so in a pattern as clear as it is compact, as explicit in its narrative as it is ornamental in its forms and colors. He has "drawn" his picture in the dark lines of lead that hold the pieces of glass together, plus a few painted brush lines fused with the glass by heating.

Stained-glass windows were designed in full scale on paper or some other flat surface; then individual pieces of glass were cut to size and laid in place over the pattern. When they were thus assembled the pieces were ready to be leaded together. Today the Chartres windows are set in demountable metal frames that can be quickly lifted down from their places by the local citizens, who are organized into brigades, each with its special assignment, to remove the windows in an emergency.

Each piece of glass was carefully selected for color and brilliance, which was determined not only by the coloring agent but by thickness and by other variations, like streaks and bubbles, that affected the passage of light. Certain irregularities, especially variations of thickness in a single piece, were inevitable because glass could not be manufactured in the large, smooth pieces we know today. (This perfection, as much as anything else, accounts for the harsh, monotonous character of second-rate modern imitations in pseudo-Gothic style.) In any light the windows of Chartres glow; in a strong light they seem almost to pulsate as the rays not only are filtered but are bent or shattered in their passage from the world outside into the dimness of the cathedral interior. A color reproduction can show some of the variations of light in individual pieces at the moment the photograph was taken, but only the living windows are subject to the minute but continuous variations of outdoor light. Even a slight change in the angle of vision brings into play millions of infinitesimal variations in refraction, giving a vibrance to the colors that in a photograph remain static. And there are the more conspicuous changes— the passing of a cloud may dim a window for a moment, while others near it seem to take on greater intensity. And at different times of day, or on different kinds of days, the glass deepens or brightens, its color sharpens or grows softer, in changing harmonies with the other windows.

Gothic Sculpture

As cathedrals continued to rise on every hand a dozen styles of Gothic sculpture developed.

15

We speak of them as schools, but often a "school" was a single sculptor working as a sort of head master of a team. Since most of the cathedrals were built over a long period of time (a notable exception is the cathedral of Amiens, built in only sixteen years), several styles might be combined in a single building, sometimes on a single portal.

The range was wide—from witty superficiality to severe formality, from acute realism to high idealism, from the grotesque and fantastic to the heavenly. This wide variety was a natural result as the Gothic world developed its cities, its commerce, its complicated society, its opposing schools of philosophy, its heretics and its reactionaries, as it fought its wars and extended its borders.

It is usual to say that Gothic sculpture reached its full expression in the thirteenth century, achieving in its own way the harmony between earthly and spiritual values that, in the pagan world, was attained in the Golden Age. And we have already said that this harmony was prefigured in the Royal Portal of Chartres, from the latter half of the preceding century. *The Virgin* (Plate B3) from a now-dismantled choir screen in the cathedral of Strasbourg may serve as an example of the culmination of Gothic harmony. She is at once a worthy Queen of Heaven and a mother so tender that even the humblest person may approach her in assurance of her compassionate love.

The Strasbourg Virgin represents one of the rare instances when the original polychromy of a statue has been preserved. The statue disappeared—as far as conclusive records are concerned—when the choir screen was demolished in 1682. After a clouded history it came to light again in 1913. It had been repainted, but this apparent misfortune was a blessing, for the original paint had thus been preserved and was almost intact under the second coat. A drawing made while the statue was in place on the choir screen shows that two angels hovering on either side supported the Virgin's veil, while the child, seated on a rosebush, offered her a

piece of fruit on which a bird had alighted.

The rosebush is a charming idea in itself, but it is also symbolical. In The Metropolitan Museum of Art *Bulletin* (April, 1949) James J. Rorimer pointed out that the rosebush is a reference to the "tree of Jesse," which traces the ancestors of Christ. In Isaiah we read, "And there shall come forth a rod out of the stem of Jesse, and a Branch shall grow out of his roots." The tree of Jesse was represented in manuscripts, in glass—in all the pictorial arts —with Christ at its top. "The connection of the

Virgin with the tree is developed in the play on the words *virgo*, Virgin, and *virga*, twig." Thus the idea of perching the Christ child on a rosebush is not just an engaging conceit but a symbolical reference. The red rosebush is also used as a symbol of the martyrdom of Christ, such symbolism here being prophetic.

This statue from Strasbourg, like other medieval sculpture, seems to reflect more than one local style. In the Middle Ages sculptors moved about from place to place, picking up new ideas from whatever sculpture they saw, influencing in turn the other wandering craftsmen who worked with them, creating countless interrelationships between local styles. A group of sculptors who worked at Rheims, for instance, moved on to Strasbourg and then doubled back to Rheims.

The Strasbourg Virgin seems to bear a double kinship to two unusual Rheims types, the *Smiling Angel* (*Figure 15*) and *The Virgin of the Visitation* (*Figure 16*). The latter, from the portal of Rheims Cathedral, should look unexpectedly familiar, for she resembles a Greek goddess or a Roman matron appearing suddenly in a Christian role. The oval face, the straight, wide-bridged nose, the small, full mouth, the low, broad brow, and the classical coiffure must certainly have had some Greek or Roman model, even if indirectly; to believe otherwise would be pushing explanation by coincidence beyond acceptable limits. But there is no evidence as to how the sculptor could have seen this model. We know that at this time French kings controlled certain areas in Greece and that there was travel to the Holy Land through Italy, but the rest is guesswork.

All guesses aside, Rheims offers a school of medieval sculpture that is specifically classical in this example and not much less so in several others. The serenity of the Strasbourg Virgin holds an echo of the ancient world; on the other hand, she has echoes too of a contrasting type that received full expression at Rheims in the *Smiling Angel*, a graceful creature with soft curls and almost overdelicate features.

Figure 13

We are a long way here from the spiritual intensity of Romanesque sculpture, from the compassionate dignity of the Royal Portal, and from the harmonious balance between earthly and spiritual values represented by the Strasbourg Virgin. Earthly values are beginning to take over; for all its entrancing loveliness, the *Smiling Angel* is more courtly than heavenly, more sophisticated than mystical. Among the aristocrats and the extremely wealthy, faith and piety were yielding more and more to the love of gracious living. The prospering middle class was becoming more and more preoccupied with creature comforts, which it could now afford, and with worldly pleasures, still sinful in theory but pleasurable indeed in practice. The *Smiling Angel* was more attractive than the angel of doom; its pretty friendliness was less demanding than the lofty reserve of the Kings and Queens of Judah; by the end of the fourteenth century even the Virgin was often represented as a charming coquette.

17

Archives Photographiques, Paris

Figure 14

Painting:
Tradition and Innovation

Stained glass, a form of painting, supplied virtually all the pictorial decoration of the Gothic cathedral. Frescoed walls and vaults, though far from unknown in the north, were most common in Italy, which had a tradition of mural decoration, in fresco and in mosaic, unbroken since Roman times. In Italy Gothic construction was not pushed to the limits it reached in France and Germany. As a rule, in spite of exceptions like the cathedral of Milan, churches remained low and had large areas of supporting wall that could be covered with pictures. Thus the demands of decoration and pedagogy that were filled in France by sculpture and stained glass could be satisfied in Italy by wall paintings.

Italian painters, like French sculptors, soon tackled the problem of realistic representation. The problems were more difficult because the painter had to rediscover the technical devices (modeling and perspective), well known to the Romans but lost over the centuries, for translating the appearance of a three-dimensional object into a representation on a two-dimensional surface.

Thus painting developed more hesitantly than sculpture. Although Cimabue painted *The Virgin with Angels* (Plate B4) well within the chronological limits of the Gothic period, it has the primitive look of Romanesque art. Even so, Cimabue was an innovator. Not much is known about him and not all scholars agree that *The Virgin with Angels* is his work. If it is not, it is the work of a close follower, one of the army of painters who appeared in Italy with the same fecundity as sculptors in the north and quickly absorbed the innovations of Cimabue and other masters who bridge the distance between Byzantine formalism and realism.

The Virgin with Angels holds to tradition in many ways—in its stiffness, its flat gold background, and the reserve of the Madonna, which makes her an object for adoration rather than a figure of mercy. But if we compare Cimabue's Madonna with one in a typical Italo-Byzantine painting, *Madonna Enthroned Between Saints Peter and Leonard* (Portfolio 9, Plate 98) we can see that the forms are softer and more graceful. There is an air of greater humanity and tenderness that must have been very striking to men of the thirteenth century, who knew only the flat, severe images that preceded it.

(By tradition, one of Cimabue's students was Giotto di Bondone, who redirected the course of painting by fulfilling the humanistic promise barely suggested by Cimabue. A single example of Giotto's painting, *Joachim's Dream* (Portfolio 8, *Figure 9*), will serve as a reminder of our previous discussions, which will be continued in the next portfolio as we follow Giotto's humanistic revolution into the Renaissance.)

It could be argued that the Christian story,

being one of miracle and majesty, is best expressed by the regal otherworldliness of the Byzantine style, that it should not be brought down to earth to be enacted by individuals close to the rank and file of imperfect mortals. This conservative and aristocratic attitude, opposed to Giotto's, was held by a school of Italian painters with its stronghold in Siena and was summarized by Duccio di Buoninsegna in an altarpiece for the city's cathedral.

The carved and gilded altarpiece was a large and elaborate freestanding structure. All that remains today is the central panel (its back and front are now separated like the two sides of a sandwich) and a scattering of smaller panels that had been incorporated beneath and above it. In the *Maestà* (*Figure 17*), the face of the central panel, the Madonna is represented in superhuman dimensions, enthroned among hosts of adoring saints. The background, in the Byzantine tradition, is gold, and gold sparkles everywhere in haloes and patterned robes. The reverse is divided into a series of small compositions telling the Passion of Christ, while other small panels on both sides of the altarpiece had scenes from the life of the Virgin. Duccio was a wonderful storyteller; each illustration not only relates an anecdote but sets the proper psychological atmosphere.

While Duccio went beyond Cimabue in softening Byzantine angularity of line and in rounding out Byzantine flatness of form, he did so to revitalize an old tradition, not to abandon it. It is always important to remember that Giotto was also painting at this time and that while we follow the course of medieval painting in the following centuries, renaissance painting is developing in another direction.

The International Style and Courtly Life

Duccio's immediate follower in Siena was Simone Martini. His *Annunciation* (Portfolio 3, Plates 31 and 32), which combines almost neurotic intensity with courtly elegance, typifies Sienese painting of this generation.

Sienese art now became a primary source of an international style of painting reflecting the sophistication of an aristocratic world dedicated to intellectualizing and to the cultivation of taste and sensibility. Art continued to serve religion, but with a change: a religious work might be treasured more for art's sake than for religion's, which explains why painting, which can be so personal, so intimate an art, took on new importance.

The Book of Hours (a private service and prayer book) illustrated by Jean Pucelle and given to Jeanne d'Évreux by her husband, Charles IV of France, is an exquisite little object measuring only $3\frac{5}{8}$ by $2\frac{3}{8}$ inches. Page after page of pictures like jewels on a strand are bordered by vivacious caprices of figure and ornament where religious association is often ignored in sheer exuberance of invention. *The Annunciation* (*Figure 18*), like several others, follows a composition of Duccio's, but whereas the Sienese master emphasized linear contours and surface patterns, this northern artist begins to model in light and shade and to create three-dimensional depth, as in the little house where the scene is set. This is a step away from the tradition of manuscript illumination as the ornamentation of a page in a book and a step in the direction of painting—that is, painting as we usually think of it, as an independent art in which the picture exists for itself. At the beginning of the fifteenth century the last step was taken in another Book of Hours, the Très Riches Heures of the Duke of Berry, illustrated by Pol de Limbourg and his brothers Herman and Jean (and completed by Jean Colombe).

The duke was one of the wealthiest and highest living members of his princely class. An avid and knowledgeable collector, he was seventy years old when he commissioned the Très Riches Heures as the crowning masterpiece of his library. Its twelve finest pages represent the months of the year, surmounted by the signs of the zodiac for the month and a

Figure 15

20

calendar for the notation of feasts and saints' days. A glance at *January* (Plate B5), which shows the duke at table, is enough to give us an idea of the staggering luxury of his life.

A chamberlain with staff and chain supervises the order of audience of various courtiers and gentlemen wearing robes of fanciful cut, elaborate turbans, rich capes, and jeweled pins. The wall is hung with a rich tapestry showing knights in battle; the table and sideboard are laden with gold plates and services. These details were not fabricated by the artist; the large boat-shaped object at the right, for instance, is the famous Salt Cellar of the Pavilion noted in the inventory of the duke's estate.

The Campin Altarpiece

The illustrations in the Très Riches Heures made great advances in realistic representation and, being essentially independent pictures, were among the manuscript paintings that helped to open the way for the great development of panel painting that now took place. The advances made by the brothers Van Eyck were discussed in the first series of Seminars (Portfolio 1, Plate 10, and Portfolio 2, Plate 16). We shall now examine a key picture in late medieval art, *The Annunciation with Donors and Saint Joseph* (*Figure 19*; detail, Plate B6), by Robert Campin, a contemporary of Jan van Eyck.

In Duccio's *Maestà* and even in statues like the Strasbourg Virgin, the Madonna is the Queen of Heaven. One school of philosophers and a corresponding school of artists insisted that she must remain so, but another school opposed this concept with one of the Virgin as a sweet and humble girl of the people. Robert Campin emphatically exemplifies this latter concept; for the first time the Annunciation is represented as taking place in an intimate domestic interior. Ordinarily it was shown in elaborate surroundings—we have seen the exquisite house in Jean Pucelle's *Annunciation*, a setting of courtly elegance and refinement be-

Figure 16

fitting an important personage. Campin departs from the tradition and paints a spick-and-span domestic interior, comfortable but far from opulent; on one side is a small informal walled garden and on the other, Joseph's workshop, with city life going on much as usual beyond the garden door and the workshop window. In her description of the picture in The Metropolitan Museum of Art *Bulletin* (December, 1957) Margaret B. Freeman, Curator of The Cloisters, quotes a fifteenth-century mystery play in which Mary says, "Here is my little room, so pretty and so neat. To serve God, my maker, and to deserve His grace, I would like to read my Psalter, one psalm after another until I have read them all." Miss Freeman also points out that Mary is obviously an impeccable housekeeper and that the "book is carefully protected even from Mary's clean hands by a white cloth. Another book and a scroll lie on the table, suggesting that she is in need of a few reference works."

These intimate and affectionate touches are rendered with the acute detail that, in Campin, is almost an obsession. We cannot always be certain where they are included for their own interest and where they are symbolical. The bench beside Mary (shown sitting on the floor to denote her virtue of humility) is decorated with two small lions. The throne of King Solomon, by tradition, was carved with lions; in the complicated analogies worked out by medieval scholars the throne of Solomon in the Old Testament was a prototype for the Virgin Mary in the New Testament. But, as the lion was also popular as a purely decorative element on furniture at this time, Campin might have included it only as a familiar detail of a city living room.

Other symbols, however, are indisputable. The lilies in the jug are a symbol of Mary's purity; the white petals enclose a golden heart representing Christ in her womb. The spotless vessel of clear water hanging in the upper left also symbolizes Mary's purity and is the equivalent of the fountain beside which she is often seated when the Annunciation is represented in a garden. The seven rays of light entering through one of the circular windows represent the seven gifts of the Holy Spirit and are thus a substitute for the more usual dove of the Holy Ghost.

In the garden just outside we come again to the red rosebush. And in the carpenter's shop we have one of the most extraordinary symbols of all—a mousetrap prominently displayed at the open window. (Another, of different design, rests on the workbench.)

The sermons of Saint Augustine give us the clue to the symbolism of this otherwise ordinary contraption: "The cross of the Lord was the devil's mousetrap; the bait by which he was caught was the Lord's death." As Meyer Schapiro has pointed out, it was believed in the late Middle Ages that knowledge of Christ's divinity had to be kept from the devil, that the devil must believe Christ to be an ordinary human being if the original sin of Adam and Eve under which all mankind suffered was to be wiped out by the Crucifixion. Christ's human flesh was a kind of disguise, the bait of the mousetrap in which the devil would eventually be caught. Thus the presence of the mousetrap at the Annunciation might be interpreted as a warning of the need for secrecy and a prophecy of the redemption of mankind through Christ.

Anderson

Figure 17

Idealism

In spite of his importance, Robert Campin's exact identity has been much disputed by scholars; some attribute certain works to him, others disagree; and some even insist that he was a painter of little merit and that the important works attributed to him are, in fact, a group of early works by another painter, Rogier van der Weyden, who may have been his pupil.

If we accept this last theory, then we must believe that Rogier changed his style drastically in his later works. Campin tells his story in familiar images, realistically detailed, relating the holy event to a bourgeois world. Rogier, on the other hand, like his Sienese predecessors, is an artist of the aristocratic style. He continues to use the traditional unrealistic golden background, the slender forms, and the patterned linear definitions that were the Sienese contributions to the international style. By these means, as in *Christ on the Cross with the Virgin and Saint John* (*Figure 20*), Rogier intensifies the ideal and spiritual nature of a scene by creating an appropriate psychological atmosphere; Campin's mundane images are spiritual only by association and through translation of the symbolism.

Rogier is the last great representative of the spiritual idealism of the Middle Ages; we could well spend more time with him here, but we must see instead one of the most extraordinary paintings of the late Middle Ages, a curiously isolated masterpiece, the *Avignon Pietà* (Plate B7), executed about 1465. No one knows who painted the *Avignon Pietà*, but the picture is obviously the work of a skilled painter and a great artist.

The body of Christ lies across the lap of the Virgin in a broken attitude speaking of the agony of the Cross. The stiff arm and twisted hand accentuate the upward-arching lines of the body, which culminate in the haloed head so tenderly supported by Saint John. Looming above the horizon of the golden sky, John's

Figure 18

face and those of the Madonna and Mary Magdalen are filled with a grief beyond human poignance, for they have witnessed the final earthly episode of a story in which their personal tragedy is dwarfed by the solemnity of man's redemption.

The Virgin and the two saints are arranged around the body of Christ in a pyramid, but the group as a whole is heavier at the right to allow for the introduction of the white-robed figure of the donor at the left. Such figures, portraits of the men who commissioned or donated the paintings, were often included as spectators at holy events—and as such they are often obtrusive. Here especially, in a scene of such high idealism, the presence of an unrelated personage could have been shattering to the mood of the picture. For several reasons, however, we accept this figure without ques-

Figure 19

tion. The donor's secondary importance is emphasized by his location to one side of an otherwise tightly integrated group and by the placement of his head below the line of the horizon, in contrast with the monumental prominence of the other heads, played against the golden sky. In the most subtle device of all, the donor alone does not gaze at the body of Christ, but raises his eyes to look a little beyond the group. Because he shares the solemnity and tenderness of the others, he is not discordant in the picture's emotional context.

The Portinari Altarpiece

About ten years later, another masterpiece fused the monumental realism of the Van Eycks and Robert Campin with the impassioned idealism of the *Avignon Pietà*, bringing to a climax the double tradition of late medieval painting. This was *The Adoration of the Shepherds* (Plate B8) by Hugo van der Goes, the central panel of a tremendous altarpiece in the usual form of a triptych with side panels that close over the central one.

The Adoration of the Shepherds presents a scheme that seems, at first, bizarre. A Virgin of monumental scale and a diminutive naked child sit within a circle of adoring figures done at differing scales. The effect of this intentionally unrational combination of forms, painted with what appears to be acutely literal detail, is to lift the scene beyond literal associations and to invest it with the quality of the supernatural, the miraculous.

The flowers in the foreground are part of an unusually complex scheme of symbolism explained in detail by Erwin Panofsky in his classic *Early Netherlandish Painting*. The scarlet lily and the iris are symbols of Christ's passion; the first represents his blood, the second the sword of grief that will pierce the heart of the Virgin as the Mater Dolorosa. The columbine is always the symbol of sorrow; here its seven blossoms specifically symbolize the seven sorrows of the Virgin.

But even without these prophetic symbols we must feel the foreboding, the resignation to ultimate anguish and sorrow, pervading a subject that is ordinarily one of joy. The fifteen angels symbolize the fifteen joys of the Virgin, yet even they adore the child in the same spirit of grief that is so moving in the Virgin's face.

Showing an adoration of the shepherds in-

24

stead of the Magi is unusual. (In the far distance, the arrival of the Magi is forecast by a member of their company who asks directions from another shepherd.) The substitution of the exotic gorgeousness and theatricality of the Magi for the piety and passionate curiosity of the simple shepherds would destroy the conception of the picture, where the child is adored not as the King of Kings but as the being who will suffer to redeem mankind. It is appropriate that the humblest of men should adore him here; the three shepherds represent three clearly individualized human beings, each experiencing in his own way the wonder and the rapture of an experience without precedent.

The eldest of the shepherds, kneeling nearest us, clasps his hands in serene joy; beside him a dark young man parts his hands in solemn wonder. The third shepherd (*Figure 21*) is a lout—snubnosed, gap-toothed, rawboned, and coarse-haired. But he is equally aware that he is in the presence of miracle, just as he will be equally the recipient of salvation through the

Figure 20

25

child. He leans forward in amazement; his face is filled with joy and reverence and almost with fright. He dares lean no closer, but his eyes start with wild curiosity as he strains forward. No head in the history of painting, of any period, surpasses this one in pyschological revelation through explicitly realistic representation.

The Adoration of the Shepherds, which was completed in 1476, half a century after Campin's *Annunciation*, brings us close to the end of the period that, in northern Europe, is still medieval. It was commissioned by an Italian, Tommaso Portinari, who represented the Medici in Bruges, as a gift to the church of the Arcispedale di Santa Maria Nuova, in Florence. Florence was the center of the Italian Renaissance, which was well under way (as we will see in our next portfolio), but *The Adoration of the Shepherds* influenced many Italian painters, not by its medievalism but by its concise, polished realism, particularly in the unidealized representation of the shepherds.

The Hunt of the Unicorn

Although we have proceeded in chronological order, it must appear that we have made some abrupt stops and starts: from one example of sculpture or painting to the next, from the idealism of the Strasbourg Virgin to the charming affectation of the *Smiling Angel*, from Sienese Byzantinism to the courtly variations of the manuscript paintings of Jean Pucelle and Pol de Limbourg, from the symbolical realism of Campin to the idealism, once more, of Rogier van der Weyden and the *Avignon Pietà*—reaching, finally, the fusion of realism, symbolism, and idealism in *The Adoration of the Shepherds*.

We have been following several threads in a complicated fabric. Now, at the very end of the fifteenth century, we pick up the courtly tradition again in one of its most attractive manifestations, the tapestries that covered the walls of the great chateaux, taking as our ex-

ample one episode, *The Unicorn at the Fountain* (*Figure 22*; detail, Plate B9), from a series of six tapestries representing *The Hunt of the Unicorn*.

We are at the edge of the Renaissance. The treatment of the subject indicates as much, for in early interpretations the unicorn was a symbol of Christ, but here it becomes also a symbol of courtly love.

The change came about through a series of reinterpretations. The unicorn has been a remarkably persistent mythological beast, one which many writers claimed to have seen with their own eyes. Four centuries before Christ it was described in Greek literature as a powerful animal that no creature, "horse nor other," could overtake. In the first century after Christ the Roman Pliny described it as a beast that could not be taken alive. As the legend grew the belief developed that the unicorn could be conquered only by a virgin; confronted by a pure maiden, he would lay his head in her lap. But in the early Middle Ages the eternally fascinating tales were adapted to the Christian symbolism of the Virgin Mary and Christ. Gabriel (the angel of the Annunciation) was identified with the unicorn's huntsman. By the time our tapestries were woven the symbolism had reverted, intermingled with its religious meanings, to one of courtly love, and it is probable that the series was woven as a wedding gift, perhaps for a couple whose initials appear interlaced in the upper right.

The scenes are full of other legendary echoes. The unicorn, who was as kindly in some tales as he was ferocious in others, was supposed to dip his horn (which was invested with all kinds of magical, medicinal, and religious properties) into streams to purify the waters of the poisons left there by malevolent beasts during the night. In *The Unicorn at the Fountain* some of these animals, a lion and lioness, a panther, a civet, a hyena, a stag, and two rabbits, stand by the stream where the beautiful unicorn dips his horn.

The hunting scenes contrast the curled locks

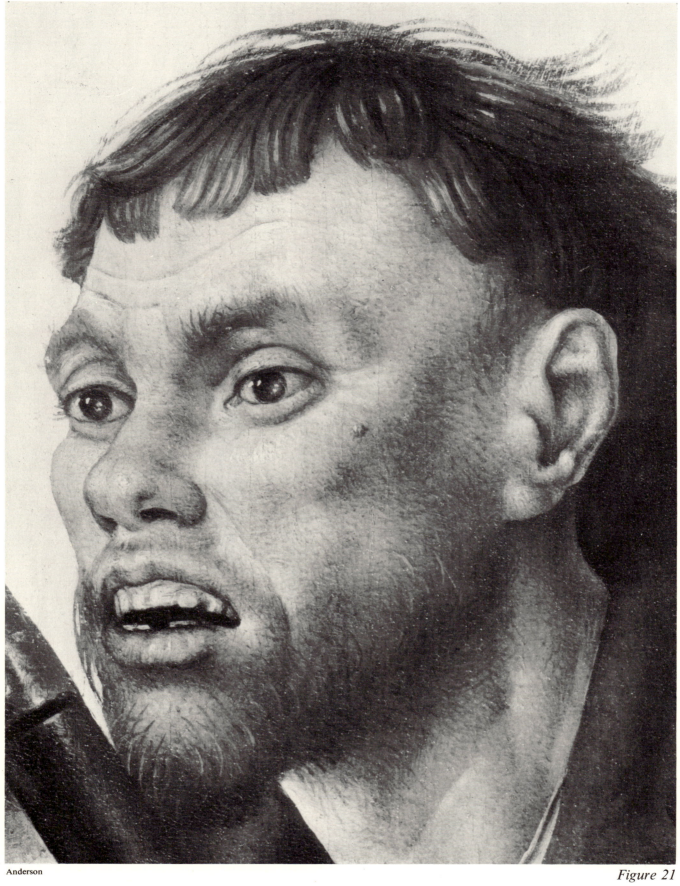

Anderson

Figure 21

and handsome faces of gentlemen wearing plumes, velvets, and brocades with the uncouth features of the beaters and other attendants. These elegant trappings, which suggest a gentleman's sport in the park of a chateau, are a glimpse of the life that was soon to form the background of the Renaissance. We have already said, however, that history is never as neat as we like to make it, and well along in the sixteenth century we find at least one picture that is the ultimate expression of a theme that haunted the Middle Ages for five hundred years—the terror and horror of death.

The Triumph of Death

In their hell scenes the earliest Romanesque sculptors showed fiends torturing the damned. At Conques a knight in mail is unceremoniously dumped from his horse to rightful punishment along with simpler souls. The Middle Ages had its full share of suffering and violence —war, famine, pestilence, massacre, and public torture. These horrid facts were combined with the subjects of an imagined hell to produce the Dance of Death, often in a series of pictures showing the mighty and the humble, the young and the old, the good and the bad,

Figure 22

as victims of the same dreaded scythe. Pieter Bruegel, who was a renaissance artist in time and, for the most part, in spirit, summarized this terror in a single awesome picture, *The Triumph of Death* (Plate B10), a panoramic holocaust painted about 1562.

In the lower right we see a lover and his mistress singing to one another, unaware for the moment that grinning Death, fiddling just behind them, has made a frightful trio of their idyllic duet. Just above, Death in the habit of a serving man offers a skull on a platter at a table from which the diners have fled, knocking over their stools. A maiden shrieks as Death the Lover embraces her, a fool tries to hide under the tablecloth, and a masked skeleton dumps wine from a cooler.

In the lower left a king lies dazed and helpless while a skeleton shows him an hourglass in which the sands have run out, while another, in stolen armor (the skeletons loved to dress in their victims' clothes), rifles his barrels of gold. A cardinal is led away by a skeleton who wears one of his confrere's hats; a starving dog nibbles at a child held in the crook of its dead mother's arm. And beyond these scenes a ravaged landscape swarms with struggling men and armies of skeletons; bloated cadavers lie about; shriveled bodies hang from gibbets; Death tolls a great bell against a horizon where smoke and flame describe universal destruction. Nowhere is there any refuge, neither on earth nor in heaven. When it was painted, Bruegel's nightmare had topical reference to the Spanish forces ravaging the Flemish countryside, but in essence it is the culmination of an important medieval theme.

The Isenheim Altarpiece

The anguish of the poverty-stricken and the diseased, the maimed and the deformed, was seldom treated in medieval art except as a subject of grotesquerie, even of cruel humor. The Dance of Death was presented with morbid relish; even Bruegel's great picture is a hor-

28

Figure 23

rifying vision of universal cataclysm at which one must shudder, not a picture that stirs one to pity for the individuals who suffer and die.

But at the end of the Middle Ages one painter who was a poet and a mystic drew upon this material for an altarpiece that is unquestioned as a supreme achievement in the art of all time. In saving it as a conclusion to this portfolio, we have violated strict chronology, for it was painted nearly fifty years earlier than *The Triumph of Death*. But it is the last supreme flowering of medieval painting, and since it represents the triumph of faith, it makes an appropriate conclusion to this survey of the Middle Ages. It is the Isenheim altarpiece, by Matthias Grünewald.

The Isenheim altarpiece is a complicated affair, opening not once as other altarpieces do, but twice, the third section having a sculptured central element. It is some eight feet high; its figures are beyond measurable dimensions in the magnitude of their power.

The Crucifixion (Plate B11), occupying the topmost panels when the wings of the altarpiece are closed, shows a dead Christ whose body has stiffened into the warped shapes of mortal agony. Every tendon is stretched or knotted; the fingers curl in final and intolerable anguish; the ugly feet, encrusted with dried streams of blood, are convulsive distortions of

twisted bone and torn flesh; everywhere, suppuration flows from decaying sores.

And yet this image is not one of horror. The initial shock of revulsion gives way to realization of tragedy and then to recognition of profound and noble serenity. And the compassionate beauty of this repellent and brutal image is undeniable when one knows that it was painted for a monastery that ministered to the victims of leprosy and venereal disease. The mortification and death of the flesh of this savior had special meaning for the souls within these putrescent bodies. But beyond that, it is the most moving symbol of the impotence of the flesh before the power of the spirit.

The divided panel of *The Crucifixion* opens to reveal miraculous joy (*Figure 23*). The morbid greens and grays and curdled reds of *The Crucifixion* give way to shafts and whorls of yellow light, to pearly clouds, rippling cloths of cherry red, skies of ringing blue, emerald leaves, and a golden porch where an angel smiles and sings. On one side is the joy of *The Annunciation*; in the center, the joy of *The Incarnation* (detail, Plate B12); then, the supreme joy of *The Resurrection*, where the rotting corpse becomes a gleaming Christ ascending through radiant light. The Isenheim altarpiece, coming at the end of the age of faith, proclaims that faith can never die.

29

Color Plates

1. THE VIRGIN AND CHILD, second half of XII century, French, School of Auvergne

   Painted oak. Height 2' 7". The Metropolitan Museum of Art, gift of J. Pierpont Morgan, 1916

2. THE STORY OF SAINT EUSTACE, lower section of Window 62, XIII century, French

   Stained glass. Cathedral of Notre Dame, Chartres

3. THE VIRGIN, 1247–52, Rhenish

   Painted limestone. Height 4' 10½". The Metropolitan Museum of Art, The Cloisters Collection, purchase, 1947

4. THE VIRGIN WITH ANGELS, last quarter of XIII century, by Cimabue (1240?–1302?), Italian

   Tempera on wood. Height 13' 11". The Louvre Museum, Paris

5. JANUARY from the Très Riches Heures of the Duke of Berry, about 1413–16, by Pol, Jean, and Herman de Limbourg (late XIV–early XV century), Franco-Flemish

   Illumination. Height 9¼". The Condé Museum, Chantilly

6. Saint Joseph from right wing of THE ANNUNCIATION WITH DONORS AND SAINT JOSEPH, third decade of XV century, by Robert Campin (active by 1406, died 1444), Flemish

   Oil on wood. Height shown 15¾". The Metropolitan Museum of Art, The Cloisters Collection

7. PIETÀ, about 1465, French, School of Avignon

   Oil on wood. Height 5' 3¾". The Louvre Museum, Paris

8. THE ADORATION OF THE SHEPHERDS, center panel of the Portinari altarpiece, about 1476, by Hugo van der Goes (active by 1467, died 1482), Flemish

   Oil on wood. Height 8' 3½". The Uffizi Gallery, Florence

9. Detail from THE UNICORN AT THE FOUNTAIN, late XV century, French or Flemish

   Tapestry. Height shown 7' 6½". The Metropolitan Museum of Art, The Cloisters Collection, gift of John D. Rockefeller, Jr., 1937

10. THE TRIUMPH OF DEATH, about 1562, by Pieter Bruegel the Elder (active by 1551, died 1569), Flemish

    Oil on wood. Height 46". The Prado Museum, Madrid

11. THE CRUCIFIXION, center panels (outer wings closed) of the Isenheim altarpiece, completed 1515–16, by Matthias Grünewald (about 1480–1528), German

    Oil on wood. Height 8' 9⅞". Unterlinden Museum, Colmar

12. Detail from THE INCARNATION, center panels (outer wings open) of the Isenheim altarpiece, completed 1515–16, by Matthias Grünewald (about 1480–1528), German

    Oil on wood. Height shown 48½". Unterlinden Museum, Colmar

Figures in the Text

1. VAULT OF THE CHOIR, XIII century, cathedral of Saint Peter, Beauvais

2. COWARDICE, medallion from side of the Portal of the Saviour, XIII century, cathedral of Notre Dame, Amiens

3. THE PENTECOST, tympanum of the narthex, XII century, church of the Madeleine, Vézelay

4. Detail of Figure 3

5. THE LAST JUDGMENT, tympanum of the west portal, XI century, church of Saint Foy, Conques

6. Detail of Figure 5

7. ACANTHUS-LEAF CAPITALS, before 1206, from the cloister of the abbey of Saint-Guilhem-le-Désert

   The Metropolitan Museum of Art, The Cloisters Collection, purchase, 1925

8. CAPITAL: SINNERS CAST INTO THE MOUTH OF HELL, before 1206, from the cloister of the abbey of Saint-Guilhem-le-Désert

   The Metropolitan Museum of Art, The Cloisters Collection, purchase, 1925

9. THE ROYAL PORTAL, second half of XII century, cathedral of Notre Dame, Chartres

10. KINGS AND QUEEN OF JUDAH, detail of Figure 9

11. Detail of Figure 10

12. WEST FAÇADE, XII, XIII, and XVI centuries, cathedral of Notre Dame, Chartres

13. CHOIR, XII century, from the church at Saint-Benoît-sur-Loire

14. FLYING BUTTRESSES OF THE APSE, late XIII century, cathedral of Notre Dame, Paris

15. SMILING ANGEL, from The Annunciation group on the side of the central portal, XIII century, cathedral of Notre Dame, Rheims

16. THE VIRGIN OF THE VISITATION, from side of the central portal, XIII century, cathedral of Notre Dame, Rheims

17. THE MAESTÀ, 1308–11, by Duccio di Buoninsegna (about 1255–1319), Italian

    Tempera on wood. Height 6' 10½". Cathedral Museum, Siena

18. THE ANNUNCIATION from The Hours of Jeanne d'Évreux, 1325–28, by Jean Pucelle (active by 1319), French

    Illumination. Height 3⅜". The Metropolitan Museum of Art, The Cloisters Collection, purchase, 1954

19. THE ANNUNCIATION WITH DONORS AND SAINT JOSEPH

    See under Plate 6

20. CHRIST ON THE CROSS WITH THE VIRGIN AND SAINT JOHN, about 1450, by Rogier van der Weyden (about 1400–1464), Flemish

Oil on wood. Height 5′ 10½″. The John G. Johnson Collection, Philadelphia

21. Head of a shepherd from THE ADORATION OF THE SHEPHERDS
See under Plate 8

22. THE UNICORN AT THE FOUNTAIN
See under Plate 9

23. THE ANNUNCIATION, THE INCARNATION, THE RESURRECTION, left wing, center panels, and right wing of the Isenheim altarpiece
See under Plate 12

Glossary

ABACUS. A flat block forming the uppermost part of a capital

APSE. A recess in a building, usually semicircular and covered with a half-dome. In a church or cathedral, the semicircular end of the choir

BUTTRESS. A masonry support built against a wall to counterbalance the lateral thrust of an arch or vault. A flying buttress is an arch or series of arches that carries the thrust over the side aisles to the piers.

CAPITAL. The head of a column or pilaster. Usually decorated

CHOIR. The part of a church or cathedral reserved for the clergy and choir. It occupies the space between the transept and the apse.

CLOISTER. A monastery or convent. Also, a covered passage, usually colonnaded, on the side of a court

COLUMN. A vertical circular support consisting of a base (sometimes omitted), a shaft, and a capital

FAÇADE. Usually the front of a building with the main entrance. Also, another side when given emphasis by architectural treatment

LINTEL. A horizontal supporting beam spanning an opening

NARTHEX. A porch, generally colonnaded or arcaded, forming the vestibule of a church

NAVE. From *navis*, ship, an early symbol of the Church. The main part of a church, between the chief entrance and the choir, separated by piers from the side aisles

PEDIMENT. The triangle (gable) at the end of a building, formed by the sloping roof. Also, an ornamental feature of this character

PIER. A vertical, non-circular masonry support more massive than a column. A compound, or clustered, pier is composed of several parts, from each of which springs one or more ribs.

PILASTER. An engaged rectangular shaft projecting from a wall, treated like a column with a base and a capital

PILLAR. A general term used for any vertical, isolated support. Also, a commemorative shaft

RIB. A masonry arch, usually molded, forming the framework of a vault

SPANDREL. The triangular space between the outer curve of an arch and the enclosing right angle. Also, the space between the outer curves of contiguous arches and a horizontal line above

THRUST. The outward force exerted by an arch or vault

TRACERY. Ornamental stonework decorating a window and holding the glass in place. Particularly characteristic of Gothic buildings

TRANSEPT. The arm of a cruciform church at right angles to the nave

TYMPANUM. The space over a doorway enclosed by the lintel and the arch

VAULT. An arched ceiling of stone, brick, or concrete. A barrel vault is semicylindrical. A groined vault is formed by two barrel vaults intersecting at right angles. A ribbed vault consists of light masonry supported by a framework of ribs. A dome is a hemispherical vault.